CHRISTMAS

SATB and piano or brass quintet, percussion, and organ

W0081671

OXFORD

Christmas Fantasy

Michael Higgins

OXFORD
UNIVERSITY PRESS

Great Clarendon Street, Oxford OX2 6DP,
United Kingdom

Oxford University Press is a department of the University of Oxford.
It furthers the University's objective of excellence in research, scholarship,
and education by publishing worldwide. Oxford is a registered trade mark of
Oxford University Press in the UK and in certain other countries

© Oxford University Press 2025

Michael Higgins has asserted his right under the Copyright, Designs
and Patents Act, 1988, to be identified as the Composer of this Work

First published 2025

Impression: 1

ISBN 978-0-19-357810-4

Music and text origination by Katie Johnston
Printed in Great Britain on acid-free paper by
Halstan & Co. Ltd, Amersham, Bucks.

Contents

Duration: 10 minutes

Composer's note

Christmas Fantasy was commissioned by the wonderfully supportive Wimbledon Choral in 2020 during the second Covid-19 lockdown. It soon became apparent that rehearsals wouldn't take place in person but, thankfully, there was a tiny window of opportunity for the members to come together in small groups to record one movement each for an online Christmas concert conducted by Neil Ferris. A live performance planned optimistically for the following year was also cancelled due to pandemic restrictions.

The carols selected reflect the joys of being together with friends and loved ones to celebrate the festive season, and hopes for brighter times ahead. I have written my own text for 'Carol of the Bells' and my own translation for 'O Christmas tree', and at the very end of the piece there's a nod towards the chaos experienced when trying to sing 'together' online.

First performed live by Wimbledon Choral, conducted by Joanna Tomlinson, with Michael Higgins (piano), at St Paul's Church, Southfields, London, on Saturday 17 December 2022.

This note may be reproduced as required for programme notes.

Instrumentation

2 trumpets in B♭
horn in F
trombone
tuba
timpani
percussion—1 player (side drum, glockenspiel, suspended cymbal, tubular bell)
organ

Full scores and instrumental parts are available on hire/rental.

If required, the work may also be accompanied by piano, playing from the vocal score.

with grateful thanks to Neil Ferris and Wimbledon Choral, Christmas 2020

Christmas Fantasy

1. Deck the hall

Trad. Welsh
arr. **MICHAEL HIGGINS**

OXFORD UNIVERSITY PRESS, MUSIC DEPARTMENT, GREAT CLARENDON STREET, OXFORD OX2 6DP
The Moral Rights of the Composer have been asserted. Photocopying this copyright material is ILLEGAL.

Fill the mead cup, drain the bar - rel, *fa la la la la la la la la.*

Troll the an - cient Christ - mas ca - rol, *fa la la la la,____ fa la la la la.*

mf

p

fa la la la la,_____ fa la la la.

While I sing of beau-ty's trea-sure,

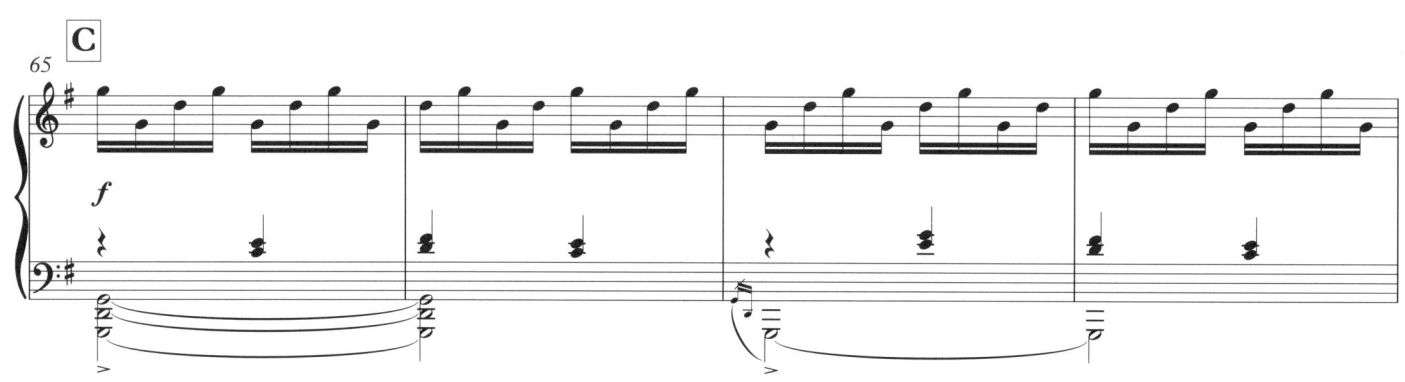

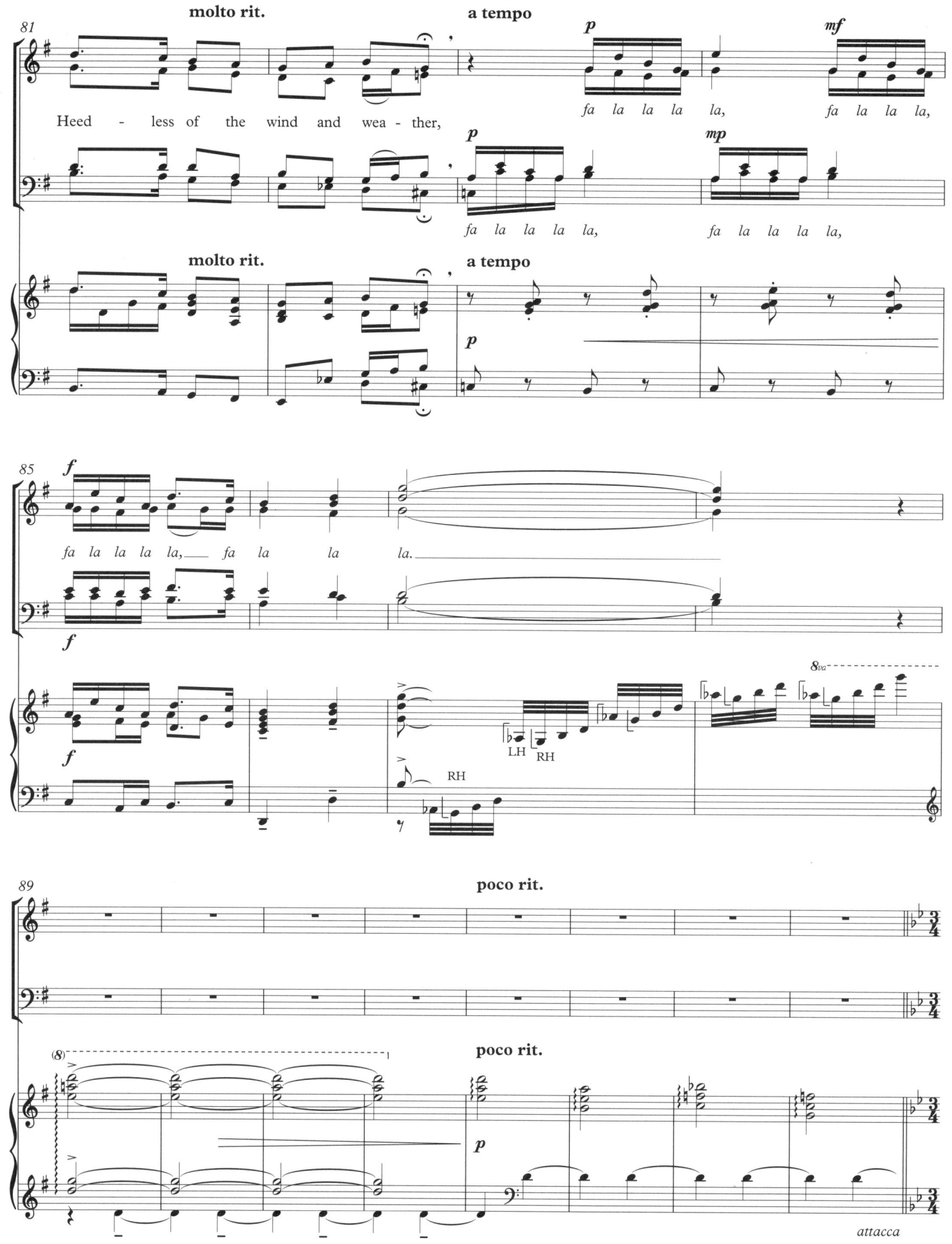

Heed - less of the wind and wea - ther,

fa la la la la,   fa la la la la,

fa la la la la,   fa la la la la,

fa la la la la,____ fa la la la la.____

attacca

2. *Carol of the Bells*

Michael Higgins

Trad. Ukrainian
arr. **MICHAEL HIGGINS**

Ring, hap - py bells, joy - ful - ly chime

* close straight to *ng* throughout

* close straight to *ng* throughout

56
mf
New Year draws near. Ring wild bells, let them ring, e - cho - ing, all
dong. Ring wild bells, let them ring, e - cho - ing, all
dong, ding dong, ding, ding
dong, ding dong, ding, ding
60
f
night they sing songs of joy, songs of love, sound - ing o'er
night they sing songs of joy, songs of love, sound - ing o'er
dong. Songs of joy, songs of love, sound - ing o'er
dong. Songs of joy, songs of love, sound - ing o'er

for all to hear.

for all to hear. With ev-'ry chime new joys ap-pear, sounds of__ hope for all to hear.

meno mosso ♩ = 66

Ding dong,_____ ding dong.*_____

Ding dong,_____ ding dong.*_____

Ding dong,_____ ding dong.*_____

Ding dong,_____ ding dong.*_____

meno mosso ♩ = 66

attacca

* Stay on the open vowel, closing to *ng* on the final quaver.
† Play small notes if required for support.

3. O Christmas tree

Ernst Anschütz (1780–1861)
trans. Michael Higgins

Trad. German
arr. **MICHAEL HIGGINS**

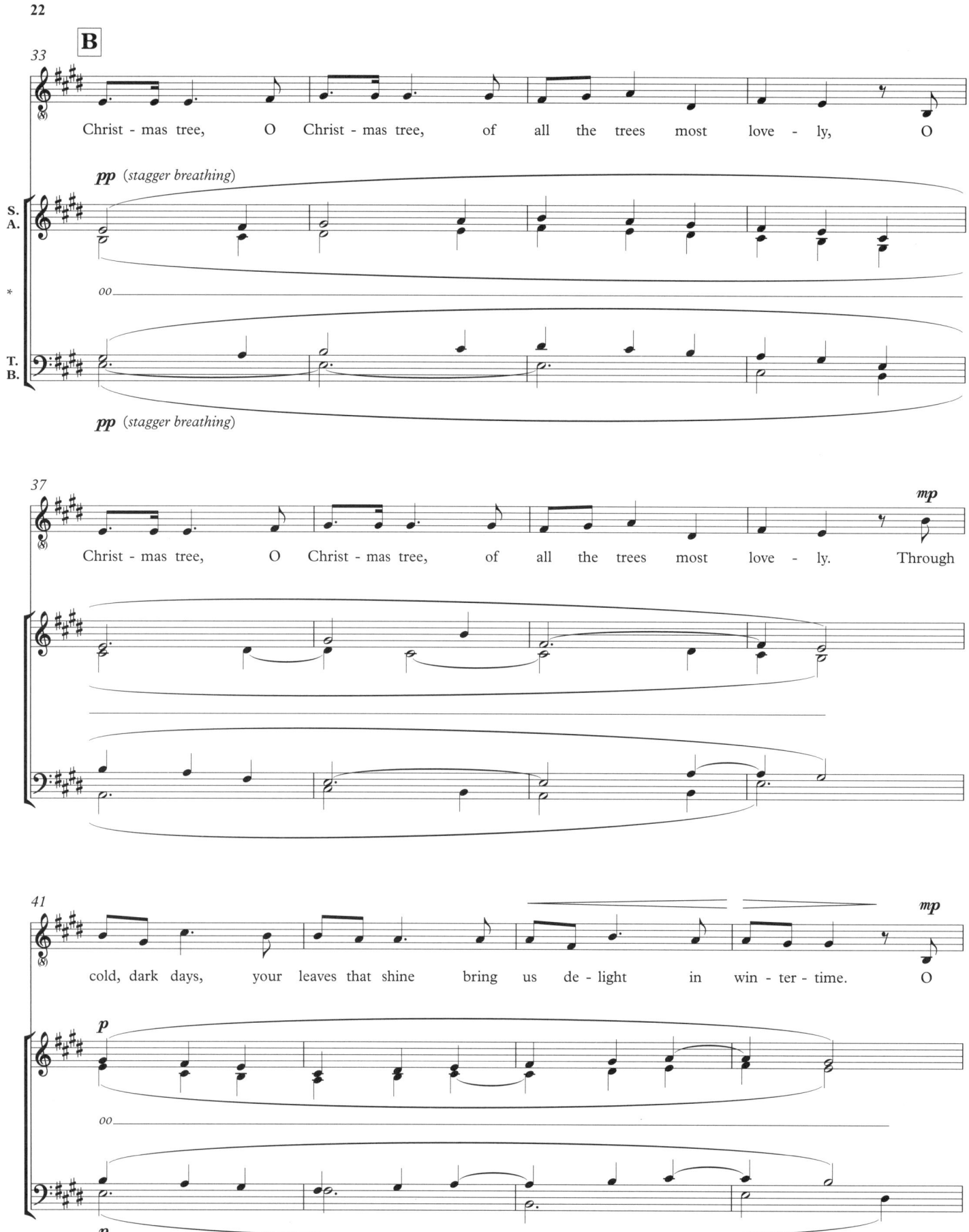

B

33

Christ - mas tree, O Christ - mas tree, of all the trees most love - ly, O

pp (stagger breathing)

S.
A.

* *oo* _____

T.
B.

pp (stagger breathing)

37

Christ - mas tree, O Christ - mas tree, of all the trees most love - ly. Through

mp

41

cold, dark days, your leaves that shine bring us de - light in win - ter - time. O

mp

p

oo _____

p

*The choral lines may be doubled on the piano if desired for bars/measures 33–48.

attacca

4. Here we come a-wassailing

Trad. English, adap.

Trad. English
arr. **MICHAEL HIGGINS**

you, and to you your was - sail too, and we wish____ you a hap - py, a

hap - py New Year, and we wish you a hap - py New

Year.____

unis. *mf*

Call

hap - py, a hap - py New Year, and we wish you a hap - py New

Year.

B poco rit. meno mosso ♩. = 69

Good mas - ter and good

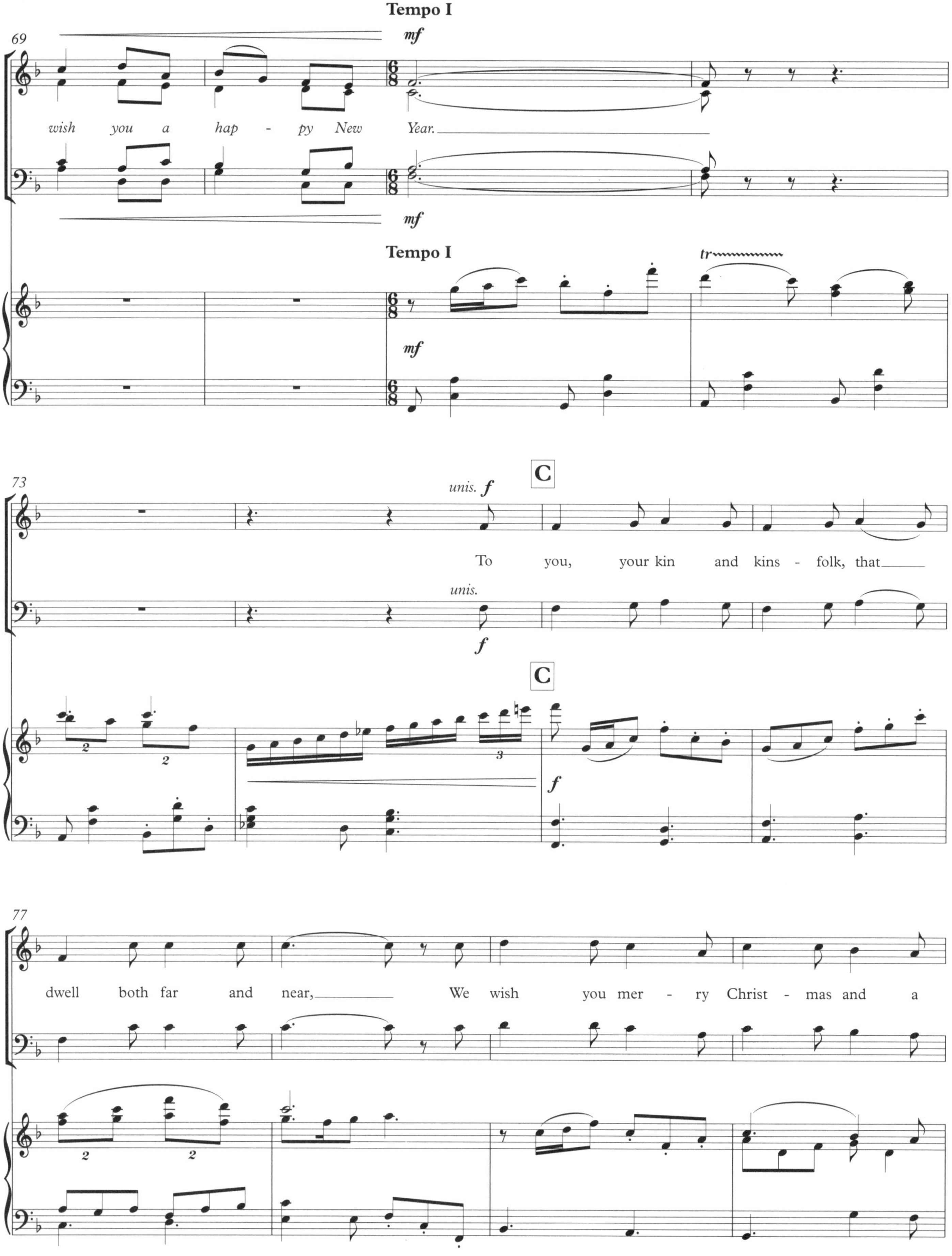
Tempo I
69
mf
wish you a hap - py New Year.
mf
Tempo I
tr
mf
73
unis. f
C
To you, your kin and kins - folk, that
unis.
f
C
f
77
dwell both far and near, We wish you mer - ry Christ - mas and a

81

hap - py New Year: Love and joy come to you, and to

85

you your was - sail too, and we wish_____ you a hap - py, a

89

hap - py New Year, and we wish you a

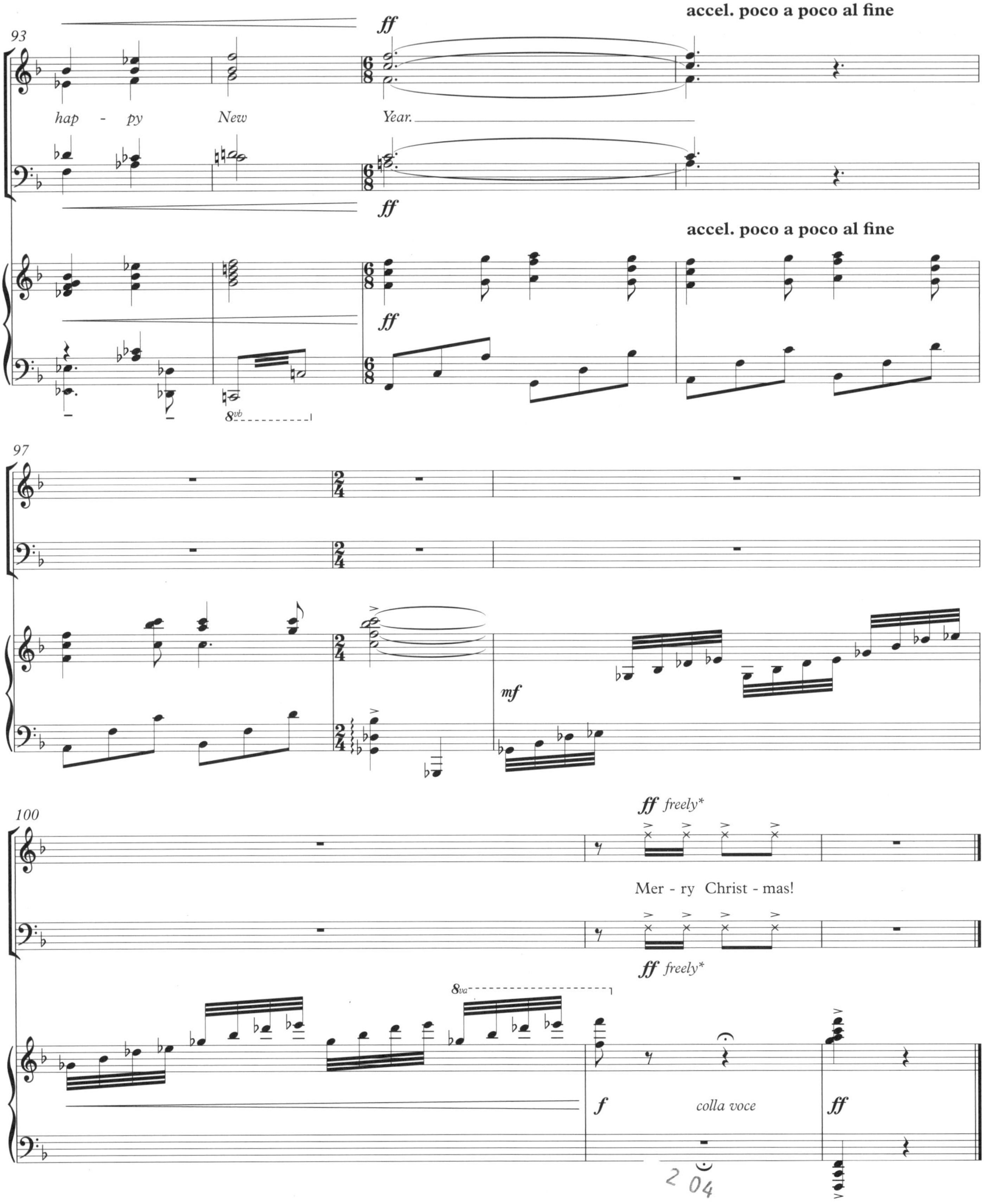

accel. poco a poco al fine

accel. poco a poco al fine

hap - py New Year.

Mer - ry Christ - mas!

* Each singer should shout the written rhythm, but starting at slightly different times.

X939 Christmas Fantasy HIGGINS

ISBN 978-0-19-357810-4

9 780193 578104